FOUR *Seasonal* TREES

GWENDOLYN KELLER

ISBN: Softcover   978-1-5035-3894-8
        Hardcover   978-1-5035-3896-2
        EBook   978-1-5035-3895-5

Rev. date: 01/27/2015

To order additional copies of this book, contact:
Xlibris
1-888-795-4274
www.Xlibris.com
Orders@Xlibris.com

My book *Four Seasonal Trees* is dedicated to my daughter, the late Keian' Monique Blunt (1975–1995), for her beauty; humility; beautiful, bright smile; love for her child, Tavon; and her thirst for living life to its fullest. I know she is smiling brightly from heaven on this wonderful and exciting accomplishment I have achieved. Additionally, my father, the late Rene Keller Sr., who encouraged his children to achieve whatever we set our minds on achieving. My father was a man who instilled great morals and values into the lives of his eleven children. I love and miss them both. Eternal rest!

ACKNOWLEDGMENTS

First, I would like to thank my Lord and Savior, Jesus Christ, for giving me the courage, confidence, wisdom, and guidance to take on this dedicated journey of achieving a sense of writing, exploring, and becoming an active author. Next, I would like to thank my parents, Helen P. Keller, and the late Rene Keller Sr. These individuals have showered me with great love, values, and morals that allotted me to accomplish whatever I set my mind on. They always gave me never-ending love and consistency.

To Warren, my handsome and outgoing son, and my handsome grandson, Tavon, I cannot express how I feel for all the love and support you have given me. My motivational and inspirational journey only expressed that all things are possible when you trust and believe in God, God's words, and yourself. To my brothers, Rene Jr. and Ron Sr., and eight beautiful sisters—Barbara, Brenda, Helen, Cheryl, Evelyn, Althea, Myra, and Terrace—countless thanks for supporting me and understanding why I had to leave early from family events. Thanks for always having my back and being lifters of my falling head. I love you.

I would like to acknowledge my beautiful daughter-in-law, Danyelle D. Blunt, and her son, Dernelle Brown, to my family.

NATURE SE4SONS

Four Seasonal Trees

There are four different seasons. They are winter, spring, summer, and fall. All have their own unique feature. Each one of them makes trees look different.

6

Winter is a challengeable season trees. Winter is very, very cold and wet. The winter season would make the colorful leaves leave their branches. The leaves lose their strength and become weak. The tree becomes bared. All the leaves are gone. It only has grayish branches and a peeling tree trunk. It looks lonesome. No one notices them. It is as if you can hear them crying in the wind, "Help up, please do not leave us alone!"

O dear winter, why you feel so near?
You make my leaves wiggle left to right,
Blowing them down to the cold, wet ground;
You are so cold!
Leaving me bared and feeling unbearable,
O do I long for summer to come,
Where I can be dressed with colorful
green leaves and happy.

8

Then spring steps in. The spring season is somewhat tricky. At certain time of the day, the weather is warm. You can plant flowers on the warm days, and other days, it can be very cold, where you need a coat and have to cover up the flowers. This tricky season allows the leaves to start falling and turning colors. The color turns from beautiful green to yellow, orange, auburn, and then a crispy brown.

Spring, you are okay!
I take you over winter.
You make my leaves become such beautiful
colors that my eyes can see clearly.
I love the colors: orange, red, and yellow, but when my leaves begin
to turn that old crispy brown, then I know what comes behind.
Spring, you are okay!

Gwendolyn Keller

The summer season brings about sunny and bright weather. Summer temperature is around seventy degrees to one hundred degrees, depending on the different states. Yet it can be breezy and shaded. The sun gives trees the nutrient it needs to grow. Take for instance, in the summer, trees are very beautiful. The leaves are green, shiny, and full. You can sit under the tree and enjoy the fresh air and the sun that shines through them.

Summer, summer, where are you?
Winter, spring, and fall are blocking your beautiful call.
I love you, summer, because I can play all day long.
I can be shade for people having a picnic or
for the birds to sit and chip away.
O dear summer, how I love for you.
Come soon and never go away.
Come so we can be happy and free.
Come so we can receive our beautiful green leaves once again,
O dear summer!

Fall is the last of the four seasons. It can be called autumn. Fall is tricky like spring. Fall days are short, and nights are long. Fall has bad weather, like heavy rain and strong winds. This season makes the trees lose all their colorful leaves. You can hear the trees crying, "Don't leave us alone! Do not go away. No, do not go away. We want to be happy and free like summer and spring!" But fall has to wait for the next season.

Gwendolyn Keller

Fall, you are the cousin of winter

You two have almost the same features.

You bring bad weather, where I become cold and wet.

No whispering sounds from the blue bird and red bird.

12

At time the old bad weather you
bring would split me into half,
and then I cry because that's the
end of me.
O fall, stay away!
Stay far, far away.
Go and be with winter so we can
have only summer and spring.

Now what is so important about the four seasonal trees is that they are recyclable. Each season, they will do the same thing. It is like the washing machine, spinning round and round. The leaves will be a beautiful green, and then the leaves turn red, orange, yellow, and crispy brown. Later, they will start falling to the ground, and afterward, all the leaves will be gone, and the tree branches and tree trunk gray.

First-Line Index

Dr. Gwendolyn Marie Keller is an early childhood teacher specializing in child psychology and development. Her partake is identifying children development via four special phases: social/emotional, physical, cognition, and language art development. Dr. Keller is sensitive to the needs of young children combined with the ability to establish a positive relationship with parents and other professionals. Dr. Keller's desire is to write many more award-winning books for children. Dr. Keller is the proud mother of two dynamic children, Warren Blunt, and the late Keian Blunt, and one grandson, Tavon Coleman. She resides in Marrero, Louisiana.